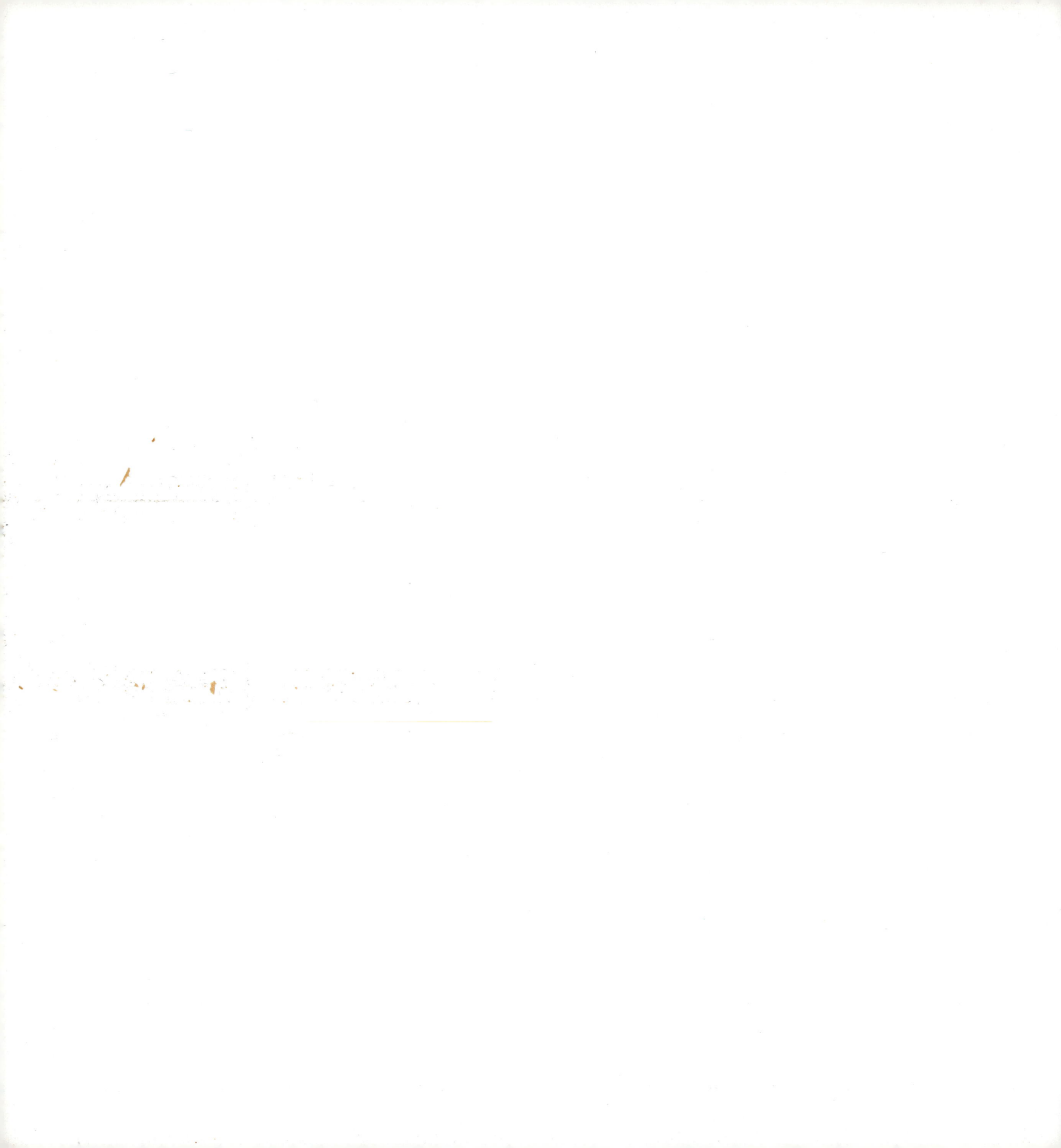

Kalaupapa In Poetry

By Takayuki Harada

Photo on back cover & inside front cover used with permission by Stanley Raymond

All other photos by Takayuki Harada
ISBN 978-0-9844458-0-6

Library of Congress Cataloging-in-Publication Data

Harada, Takayuki.
Kalaupapa in poetry / by Takayuki Harada.
p. cm.
ISBN 978-0-9844458-0-6 (pbk. : alk. paper)
1. Leprosy--Patients--Poetry. 2. Kalaupapa (Hawaii)--Poetry. I. Title.
PS3608.A7246K35 2010
811'.6--dc22
2010028480

First Printing, September 2010

Scripta
1215 Center Street, Suite 210
Honolulu, Hawaii 96816
Ph: (808) 732-1709
Fax: (808) 734-4094

Printed in Korea

Dedication

This book is dedicated to Paul Tadashi Harada who died on January 4, 2008, and to the more than 8,000 other Hansen's disease (leprosy) patients who lived and died in Kalaupapa. It was their love and sacrifice that made it possible for families and relatives throughout the state of Hawaii to live a life free of prejudice and stigma. This book is also dedicated to Winnie Harada and to all of the other patients who continue to reside in Kalaupapa and throughout the state of Hawaii.

Acknowledgments

An appreciation to Gwyn Mihara, for her generous time and effort in putting all of the material together for publishing, to my sister, Fumiko Hashimoto, who read and provided corrections to the manuscript, to Valerie Monson, a friend who provided invaluable comments to the final product, and to all who encouraged me to publish this book.

Foreword

Taka Harada's deep and sensitive love of Kalaupapa and its people shine through every page of his poetry. His heart vibrates with the breath of Kalaupapa in a most amazing way. About three years ago, my wife, Diane, and I along with Taka and his wife, were privileged to visit Taka's brother Paul and his wife and the island that had been his home. It proved to have been one of the most moving and penetrating experiences of our lives.

It would be difficult to visit this place called Kalaupapa and not be touched and changed by its poignancy, beauty and the grace of its loving and forgiving people. The people of Kalaupapa found an abiding and deep love and faith that sustained them through what others would consider to be horrific and devastating circumstances.

The deep love and faith that Taka writes about is a result of his observing and experiencing Paul's amazing transformation over the years and the profound spiritual opportunity to experience just a little of what I felt in this magic place. Take time to experience a sacred space through Taka's eyes, ears and heart and allow yourself to experience a sacred space through his poetry and photographs. There are few places in the world where one is touched so deeply. This, the land of Father Damien, is truly one of those places.

Jerry Jampolsky, M.D.
Co-author of "A Mini Course For Life"

Introduction

In 1963, I was visiting friends in Kaunakakai ("Topside"), Molokai. I contacted my brother, Paul, in Kalaupapa to say hello. He invited me and my friends to visit him there. A nurse and friend of our host suggested we accept his invitation. At that time, we were young so we decided to walk down the steep, winding trail to the settlement.

Early the next morning our host drove us to the lookout to begin our hike down the trail. It was a daunting task to hike down the steep cliff leading to the Kalaupapa peninsula. However, the vistas of the ocean, beaches and the settlement itself were spectacular. Today, one can take the mule trail down to the settlement. Both Kalawao and Kalaupapa were perfect places to isolate the sick and disabled who were afflicted with leprosy. They could hardly be expected to climb the formidable cliffs to freedom. It was the only way out of the peninsula, other than by boat or ship.

On January 6, 1866, King Kamehameha banished the first load of patients to the desolate peninsula. Patients and their *kokua* (helpers) had to fend for themselves on the wind-swept and forbidden land. Thus began a part of Hawaiian history that is both shameful and poignant. If a lesson is to be learned from this banishment, it is about ignorance, prejudice and most importantly, compassion towards one's fellow man.

In 1963, my personal odyssey with Kalaupapa began. The powerful *mana* of the land drew me back for many visits and Kalaupapa has become an important part of my life. I read much of the history of Kalaupapa. I fell in love with her and her people, many of whom have gone on to be with the Master they served. I have often shared her with friends so they too can experience the inexplicable feeling of peace and well-being that pervades the settlement and can come away better citizens of humankind.

I have written my reflections of Kalaupapa in this collection of essays and poems of the place and the people who inspired me, especially Paul and Winnie Harada. On July 21, 1995, the return of the relic of Father Damien and the celebrations which took place that day, left a powerful impression and moved me to write about that day.

Father Damien and later, Brother Dutton and Mother Marianne, were individuals who made their impact on the patients because of their compassion and love for their fellow man. Father Damien, who ministered so untiringly with the leprosy patients, finally succumbed to the disease and died in April 1889. He was buried next to the church in Kalawao. His remains were later exhumed and returned to Louvain, Belgium, where he first entered religious life. An effort to return him to the land he loved culminated in the return of one of his hands. The "Relic of Blessed Damien," was returned to Kalawao for burial on July 21, 1995. The opportunity to witness the celebration of the return of the "Relic of Blessed Damien" inspired me to put to paper my feelings of that day. I was honored to be part of the powerful spiritual atmosphere created by the return of Damien to his people in Kalaupapa.

I shared this with my family and they encouraged me to have it published, especially my sister, Fumiko. I had further encouragement to do so by other friends and family who read the manuscripts. Dr. Ellen Caringer, Dr. Gerald Jampolsky and Dr. Diane Cirincione, thought it should be shared by having it published. I am humbled by their encouragement to share these reflections of my innermost feelings and thoughts so that other people could learn more about this very special place.

I'd like to dedicate this to my brother Paul Harada and his wife, Winnie, my wonderful hosts during my visits to this very special place. They taught me to be always compassionate and loving without prejudice or fear.

The Arrival of the Relic of Blessed Damien

St. Francis Catholic Church, Kalaupapa

It was the end of a beautiful day. God brushed the skies as the sunset and dusk approached. The cool trade wind breezes blew softly over the settlement. Everything was perfect for the return of Damien, the Blessed. The long-awaited "event of the century" arrived. This was a long anticipated moment. For each person, preparing for this evening was a private and special process.

I grew nervous and excited. I stood outside the church videotaping the evolving scenes around me. I could feel the powerful energy of this great man who was "returning home." I could not remain still. My thoughts drifted from moment to moment. I was in such awe of this occasion.

Paul and I had visited the church earlier that day while Winnie helped decorate it. It was beautifully decorated, simple yet so elegant. That so many of the flowers were from Paul's garden made it even more special for me. Having earlier discussed the permissibility of my location with Paul, I positioned myself in the balcony of the church to observe the arrival of Damien's relic during that evening service.

The choir of the St. John Vianney Church of Kailua, Oahu, presented a concert as the people awaited the arrival of Damien. As the choir started, I was overwhelmed by a tremendous sense of worship; a feeling that permeated my very being. I had never experienced such awe before. It was so powerful that I trembled throughout the evening. The church was alive with the Spirit of God.

The choir sang beautifully, as if the angels of heaven descended upon the church. Song after song added to the anticipation. The church was filled with the patients and their *kokua* or helpers, who came to participate in this most private service. There were a few other "visitors" in addition to myself in the congregation, but for the most part, it was an hour set aside for the people of Kalaupapa. I sensed their intense anticipation of "their Saint." They were there to welcome him home in a very reverent and regal manner. I wished the whole world could have experienced this night.

Finally, the moment arrived! The sound of the table carrying the reliquary of Damien's hand broke the holy silence of the night - creaking as it was wheeled to the front of the church where a table was prepared to display the beautiful box in which lay the "Relic of Blessed Damien." As it came into view, a shudder ran through my body and emotions overflowed. Tears ran unchecked. It was almost too much for me to bear. It was the culmination of several months' focus on this profound event.

The congregation began to move quietly and reverently to the front of the church. Each with his or her own thoughts as deformed hands and disfigured bodies reached out to touch the box. The honor to "only touch the box" surely brought healing and peace to each participant - a touch to make one whole again emotionally, physically, and spiritually, as the one being touched.

Perhaps the most emotional moment for me was to witness Paul and Winnie standing in line and finally touching and welcoming Damien back. Paul knelt before Damien and then with two gnarled hands, welcomed him back with an embrace. It was a most moving moment. The powerful picture of the overflowing love for this man is a testament of his life's work with the "living dead." GREATER LOVE HATH NO MAN THAN THIS...I know that Paul and Winnie knew and loved him. This was truly a moment when time was no more and Damien became alive to all who witnessed this awesome event. Oh, the tears of happiness for these two whom I loved so very much.

The Hand of Damien

Peering through eyes of wonder
The hand of Damien was before me
An aura of holiness presented itself
To the congregation below
And to the observer above
All became one in the love of God
Through a man dedicated to mankind.
It did not matter what his estate in life
He saw infinite worth of flesh and spirit.
This physical hand overwhelmed me
God touched me in a special way
For the moment, and the moments to follow.
How touching as other men touched him in return
To feel from memories of his work
To receive the spirit of his Master's love
To care, to see beyond the flesh
To heal spirit, life, emotions, scars,
Each participant's life changed and refreshed
What a legacy to this man whose hands did so much!
God spoke in an ever silent and loving way,
"Remember this moment as you witness this occasion
When I presented to you the Hand of Blessed Damien, My servant."

V. C. J. S.

Sacred to the Memory
of the Rev.d Father
DAMIEN DEVEUSTER
Died a Martyr to the Charity
for the afflicted Lepers
April 15, 1889.

R. I. P.

Damien

Solitude and pain were his companions,
Walking the path of the Suffering Servant.
How difficult to fathom the great sorrow he felt,
The lost and aimless lives he encountered,
No hope for the morrow and only sadness for the day.
The rocky and windswept plains of Kalaupapa,
So much like the barren and dusty hills of Jordan,
The same hills that his Christ trod for a lost humanity.
The hidden broken lives obscured by human prejudice,
Or by the uncaring and unloving spirits of the world.
Lives shattered and literally disintegrating,
Such horrible scenes witness to society's inhumanity.
His mind opened to the wisdom of God.
His ears heard the cries halfway around the world.
His eyes beheld the needs of pitiful human tragedy,
His mouth spoke words of comfort and love for his adopted flock.
His hands unafraid to touch the vilest of human flesh.
His heart molded by the Master's loving touch of compassion.
His feet walked where need resided and cries were unheeded.
The richness of earth comes from souls like his,
No greater love for all the world to witness.
The crown of life was his but he did not claim it,
Oblivious to worldly fame and fortune.
He answered the Master's call to duty.
Kalawao and Kalaupapa were but a sojourn to this man of faith.
Damien, the Blessed of Kalaupapa.

Golgotha of Kalawao

The birth of a child
Promises so much to the world
A mother's love
A father's dream
Imparted upon the soul
Its destiny a promise
Only God knows.

Single mindedness
Kalawao and the leper
Each seeking the other
Misery and loneliness together
Walking hand in hand
Like lovers in love
Companions forever.

The cross was his walk
They railed him
They loved him
The paradox of the pilgrim
Whose feet and hands
Do the bidding of the heart
And not the mind.

He was popular and hated
He exceeded those above him
The suffering servant
Shining forth where neither darkness
Nor fear nor hatred could hide
The light upon the hill
The imitation of the Christ.

Golgotha upon the hill
Stood the cross
Lifting upon itself
The Burden, the Love
Itself the Sacrifice
Exalted above the earth
And the mire of human condition.

He washed their leprous wounds
The repugnant odor tolerated
Became one with his sheep
The road to Golgotha
Suffering for his fellow man
Amidst the railings of priests
And friends and leaders.

Golgotha of Kalawao
Christ was there
God was there
Love rang out
With a loving heart
Tired feet and body
Into thy hands I commend my spirit.

New birth, New life.
Golgotha of Kalawao.

Kalawao

Birds singing, the cool breezes caress each face.
Peace and stillness permeate all who stand here.
Silence broken only as ocean waves dash against the shores,
Oh, what wholeness one feels, removing all fear.

The hands of God touched this paradise,
Only He could form a place of such beauty.
Sculpturing shimmering cliffs and verdant valleys.
Where else on earth are such wonders on display?

Once so much sadness overshadowed this land.
How could paradise hold such deep, overwhelming sorrow?
So many touched her shores only to know
The painful loneliness and hopelessness of a dark tomorrow.

Could such horrible scourge blemish this perfect land?
Leprosy so destructive to the body and soul in its possession.
Helpless cries muffled by the noise of ignorance.
Separation and discrimination without reason or compassion.

Thoughtful reflection disperse dark clouds over Kalawao.
The light of sunshine illuminates the darkest human mind.
God through faith, hope and love replaces the bitter cup.
God's eternal love in this place to find.

A Hui Hou

Kalawao beckons to its children
Never to leave this place forever
It calls to all to return.
Our call to one another,
"A Hui Hou!"

The Blessed came and left
The call to heaven
The call to Belgium
Only to return again,
"A Hui Hou!"

A quiet place of refuge
To contemplate and meditate
Damien, Martyr of Molokai
Sweetness now begins to flow,
"A Hui Hou!"

We meet again
Here where his exceptional ministry began.
Blessed Damien comes back to his beloved rest
His spirit always said,
"A Hui Hou!"

Kalawao Scene

Waikolu Valley in the distance
The spirit of the land spoke today
So softly and in almost perfect silence,
In its soothing voice and calming way.
Kalawao continues to share her presence,
Giving the soul of man an oasis.
A respite from worldly nonsense,
A peaceful, loving, and spiritual quietness.

Kalaupapa

There is a unique place on this earth today,
Where life takes on a special meaning.
Natural surroundings so awesome and inspiring
Lifting trodden spirits high above the cares of the world.

Soaring above, with effortless flight in open sky,
Wings outstretched, carrying in the winds of Aloha.
Above the sun and below the rain refresh Kalaupapa
Quenching the thirst for moments of peaceful respite.

The ocean calm and crystal clear,
The air fresh and pure for all to experience.
The sounds of nature intermingled with the music of silence,
Unspoiled by the senseless and noisy clutter of the world.

KALAUPAPA, a land touched by the hand of God,
It is a restful and peaceful place.
Almost beyond belief and one day, face to face,
I'll thank God who created this land with such loving grace.

Mother Marianne Cope of Kalaupapa

On January 22, 2005, I flew to Kalaupapa to witness what I considered a very spiritual moment in the history of the settlement. It seemed so extraordinary that this tiny settlement of Hansen's disease patients would produce two persons considered for sainthood in the Roman Catholic Church. Both Father Damien and Mother Marianne Cope heeded God's call to serve the "outcasts" in this tiny settlement.

When the day to exhume the remains of Mother Marianne began, the scene changed. The moment became captive of a gentle spiritual force. As I stood there among a myriad of people, I could feel her spirit descend upon us. The rain, the trees, the birds, the ocean, and the land all seemed to respond as they bid farewell to Mother Marianne.

We all stood in awe as we experienced the holiness of that moment. It was a moment of recognition that our walk with God will be our legacy as it was, is, and will be for Mother Marianne.

The following are impressions of that moment as we became immersed in and one with the presence of holiness. It was truly a time when one's life was changed as we meditated upon what God wrought in that place and in the life of Mother Marianne.

Mother Marianne

Nestled among the stately ironwood pine trees
The winds whisper softly through the uplifted branches
A sweet song lifted up to the heavens
A lullaby for the one resting in God's presence!

Below the four corners of this ground are guarded
Areca palm trees stand tall, gracefully swaying with the breeze
Dedicated sentinels for all these many years
Guarding dutifully and peacefully this resting place!

The birds all seem restless and forlorn
Their flight and sorrowful songs fill the morning air
They sing for all creation in honor of a departing one
A simple musical symphony for a loving Saint!

The heavens open up in tearful ways
Little drops of rain intermittently fall to the earth
Baptizing this holy ground below
A rainbow arched the sky as all is well with God!

The soft cradle of the sacred ground
Embraced a saint of God within her bosom
Faithfully, silently becoming one with her
A final testament of a dedicated life to God!

Oh, what mortal, finite creatures are we
That we stand in silent meditative awe
Our utter dependence on our Creator
A reminder that He requires our best and our all!

Mountain Scene

Clouds adorn a majestic mountaintop
Waterfalls cascading from cliffs and valleys
A rainbow arching in the skies amongst the ridges
Home of the forests, birds, and animals
Unmatched sacred, beauty abounds!

Kalaupapa Scene

Mysterious veil formed by dark clouds and misty rain,
Enshrouding sheer cliffs reaching to azure skies.
Swirling winds with moisture cleanse the landscape,
Ocean waves foam and crash over rocky shores.
Waves from some distant origin,
Adding to the beautiful and inexplicable scene.

Kalaupapa Seashore

Basking in the sunshine and tranquility
A mother seal and her newly born pup
Clear cerulean blue waters lap upon the shore
Cooling both creatures as they lay together
At harmony with each other and their environment
A perfect scene of nature at peace

Song of Kalaupapa

They shared a common lot
Grief, pain, loneliness, hoplessness
Rich, poor, male, female
Young and old
It mattered not!

Humanity's spirit broken with shame
Scared and scarred
Japanese, Chinese, Portuguese
Filipino and Hawaiian
All races they came!

Facing treacherous ocean shore
Rocky, desolate, and foreboding
The terrible curse of chance
Robbing dignity and self worth
Earth's mournful lore!

Search the looming crowd for a friend
Among the frightened, staring eyes
A solitary light among the throng
God's gift of the Blessed
Healing comes to the land!

Bells ring their solemn song
One more fallen child of God
Cradled in rocky, windswept plains
A final walk in life's journey
A place where they belong!

Unmarked graves tell a story
Of their ultimate human sacrifice
Years of so much human suffering
In Kalawao and Kalaupapa
Vivid lessons of darkness and glory!

Names of each individual
Paul, Winnie, Ivy, Johnny
Rekindle the memory of this place
Names not to be forgotten
The lessons of defeat and survival!

All darkness fade and light appear
Hope rather than despair
Faith rather than skepticism
Love rather than judgment
God rather than fear!

A song so sad and melancholy
Lifted up in memory of those who came
Kalawao and Kalaupapa both
Shared with the worst and the best
Human suffering became holy!

Sunset at Oceanview

God brushed the skies over Kalaupapa,
Leaving in its wake a spiritual calmness.
The horizon struggles to maintain itself,
Scattered clouds create perfect balance.
The flawless scene captured for eternity,
Another stroke of God's eternal creativity.

Pohaku Malie

Anticipation beckons me to Pohaku Malie!
The soothing quietness evokes an eternal song.
The music - tranquil and calm - soothes the soul.
Food for the tired and the weary.

I stand on Pohaku Malie!
Gazing toward majestic cliffs of separation.
Feeling its protective presence cradling my tired spirit,
Nurturing it with renewal, comfort, strength and faith.

Shifting, sitting on Pohaku Malie!
I can feel the Creator's loving presence.
Sweet solitude and worship mixed with awe and peace,
Sharpen my spiritual senses.

I ponder the wonders surrounding Pohaku Malie!
Its beauty leads to folded hands and bended knees.
Prayerfully and reverently in awe of all that is around me.
God, reaffirm who I am as I gratefully acknowledge Thee!

Where God Lives

Where God lives, there are praises!
We who serve the Lord God,
Rejoice, rejoice.

Where God lives, there are praises!
I'll sing a song of gladness,
Because He is love.

He will keep me forever.
He will be my strength.
We who lift our voices,
Praise His Name where we are!

Where God lives, there are praises!
We who serve the Lord God,
Rejoice, rejoice!

(May be sung to music of "Hawaiian Lullaby")

This poem was inspired by my many visits to Kalaupapa, a very special place on this earth. It is where God lives and inspires praise for His Name amidst the separation of family and the permanent physical and emotional scars that were inflicted on those sent to the settlement. The patients found comfort in their God despite the suffering and isolation experienced because of human fear, ignorance and man's inhumanity to his fellow man.

I sit at my desk trying to digest the reality of the passing of Paul. I thought about this day often as word came that Paul was diagnosed with cancer. The initial diagnosis was not good although he had decided to do chemotherapy to stop the spread of the disease.

Talking to him at length about the cancer assured me that he was ready for whatever happened to him. I take much comfort in knowing that he was ready for the inevitable end that awaited him. God was never far from him and he was always within the embrace of his God. Whatever comfort and peace he had came because of his intimate relationship with God.

Knowing that Paul was ready did not mean that I was ready for this moment. It was difficult to stop the inevitable sobbing that racked my soul when Glenn said, "Paul died at 5 pm in Kalaupapa."

Paul

The evening sunset shone brightest this day
Within the rays of light was added another
For your soul shone forth its purity
As your hands reached for the heavens
Your smile radiated in the evening sky
Clothed with the winds of Kalaupapa
Together with oneness in nature
Forever eternally your light to shine!

Left behind are the tears of sadness
Yet, each tear will cleanse our soul
Your presence will never leave us
For it lives in memories that are eternal and forever
Your voice, your laughter, your effervescent nature
Became a part of all who were touched by your presence
Everyone who shared a moment with you on a sandy beach
Or by the calming sea or on a rocky shoreline!

Today you leave with us your very essence
Each with a little part of your life
A life too large for each of us to bear
Not the scars or the pain or the tears
Nor the separation nor the loneliness nor the abandonment
Not the fears or the hopelessness or the emptiness
But in your life were faith and hope and love
The gifts of your God who lifted you to the heavenly places!

This moment is a moment of true love
We have loved you from the moment we saw you
Under the mango tree in Lumahai Valley
When you came home to your birth place
To begin the long road of oneness with each of us
Though as siblings we were a little confused - but happy -
You became our brother and friend again
For all of eternity!

This is Our Home

Deep within Mother Nature
At creation's birth eons ago
The ooze, the primordial awakening
Arising from the deep chaos
This is our home!

The cataclysmic moment creating high, majestic cliffs
Angry waves and winds beat against the shore
Deep within, the violent eruption
Sea and molten lava clash in nature's way
This is our home!

Clashing is nature's way of creating
The birthing of this land so long ago
Life reaching above the cold, dark deep
Buffeting winds and rain cool the land
This is our home!

The birds look down upon the desolation
Seeds of life drift upon the shores
Life at last languishing and struggling
Persistent life goes on and on and on
This is our home!

This land now so pristine and peaceful
Untold millennia passed you by
The home of plants and birds upon the land
Fishes abound along your shores
This is our home!

Then violence sorrowful ring out upon your shores
The sad, the painful, the shameful, the soulful human cries
Humanity's greatest depravity upon one another
O death in life, O life in death
This is our home!

Once again violence and destruction upon your shores
Again, a light flickers upon the land
Amongst the guilt and shame
Hope, faith, justice, dignity, and love abound
This is our home!

The land now so pristine and peaceful
The painful memories turn to hope
A new spirit moves upon the land
Touching all life that comes to its shores
This is our home!

Because of You, I Am

Because of you, I am a better person
You have shown me the way of life
To live on common ground with those around me!

Because of you, I am able to understand
How to live with others around me
Who believe so differently from me!

Because of you, I am a better healer
It matters not who you are or what you believe
You taught me the value of every person!

Because of you, I am more loving
Your actions showed me how to love
Myself, my neighbor, and my God!

Because of you, I am more inclusive
I understand the destructive ways of discrimination
And remove them from my ways!

Because of you, I am more hopeful
I could never understand utter loneliness
I still struggle to understand it fully!

Because of you, I am enlightened
I only saw things dimly through foggy lenses
Now I see clearly faith, hope and love abound!

Because of you, I am part of the world
Not despised, rejected, or discarded
But a loved, created, precious being!

Because of you, I am whole

Kalawao, Makanalua, Kalaupapa,

Mahalo!

Father Damien

Father Damien began his long pilgrimage from Belgium to the shores of Hawaii where he landed on March of 1864. His ministry and devotion to all who were sent to Kalawao and Kalaupapa on Molokai began on May 10, 1873. His exceptional commitment to his work among Hansen's disease patients and his dedication to God were truly inspirational to all. Father Damien was canonized a Saint on October 11, 2009.

About the Author

Takayuki "Taka" Harada was born in the Lumahai Valley on the island of Kauai and grew up in a taro farming family on the north shore of that island. He attended school on Kauai, later moving to the island of Maui where he raised three children and graduated with a Bachelor of Public Administration Degree from the University of Hawaii, West Oahu College. Taka has been active in numerous community organizations on Maui and currently serves as a lay pastor at Keawala'i Congregational Church in Makena, Maui where his poetry and writings have been shared in newsletters and in their publication "The Meditations of My Heart." As an active member of Ka Ohana O Kalaupapa, an advocacy group for Hansen's disease patients in Kalaupapa, his poetry has been shared in numerous venues across Hawaii as well as in Japan and Taiwan. This book was written out of his desire to share the profound experience that is Kalaupapa, its history and its people.